zendoodle coloring

Hopeful Inspirations

Other great books in the series

zendoodle coloring

zendoodle coloring

Hopeful Inspirations

Uplifting Expressions to Color and Display

illustrations by
Bonnie Lynn Demanche

ST. MARTIN'S GRIFFIN
NEW YORK

ZENDOODLE COLORING: HOPEFUL INSPIRATIONS.

Copyright © 2017 by St. Martin's Press. All rights reserved.
Printed in the United States of America. For information, address
St. Martin's Press, 175 Fifth Avenue, New York, N.Y. 10010.

www.stmartins.com

ISBN 978-1-250-14160-6 (trade paperback)

Our books may be purchased in bulk for promotional, educational,
or business use. Please contact your local bookseller or the Macmillan
Corporate and Premium Sales Department at 1-800-221-7945,
extension 5442, or by e-mail at MacmillanSpecialMarkets@macmillan.com.

First Edition: August 2017

10 9 8 7 6 5 4 3 2 1

Be prepared for the worst, but Hope for the best

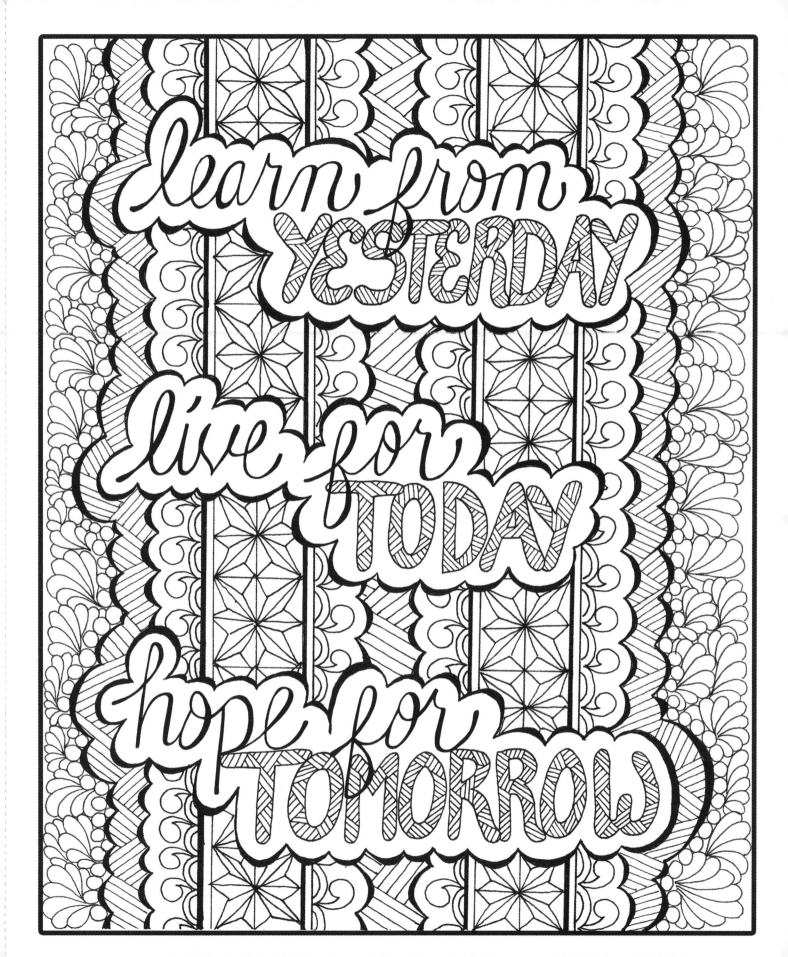

Life is not a matter of holding good cards, but of playing a poor hand well.

When the sun goes down the stars come out make a wish and never lose hope